Reflection:

Change Starts With YOU!

Joseph M. Majors

Reflection: Change Starts with YOU!

ISBN: 9781737461708

Cover: Thoughts 2 Print Press
Publisher: Thoughts 2 Print Press

Dedication

There are so many people that have supported me through all my nonsense and craziness that it's really unbelievable to me at times. So my first thank you goes to my mama because her love is beyond unconditional. If she has it to her name she has never denied me. She has given me her beautiful looks, her blunt point of view, and her zero tolerance for B.S.! All my life she has told me only the strong survive and since I've been down she always lets me know, we're doing life together. I could go on and on, but I'll just say, 'Thank you Mama.'

Next is my father because he gave me an example of the type of man and father I never want to become. He made way too many excuses. Because of him, I believe if you show me a person who always has an excuse then I'll show you someone who isn't trying their hardest.

Now to my big sister, I'm not writing this book without her being my sister. She has given me so much substance and perspective about life that has allowed me to have a better understanding about why certain things are the way they are. I love her so much for that.

My big brother is my protector and father figure. It gives you so much confidence knowing you've got someone next to you who will give their all for you. Through his vantage point I was able to see that if you position and carry yourself a certain way there is nothing or no one that can touch you.

My daughter Journee is my heart. Even though she was brought into this world in not so ideal circumstances, I wouldn't trade her for the world. She's the reason I HAD TO CHECK MY REFLECTION. There's no way I can allow her to see the person I was before my bid as her father.

I would also like to thank Cousin Maurice, Cedric, Courtney, Greg, Aunt Carla, my bro DeMarcus, Tiffany, Neka, Jessica, my nieces Breonna and Bria, and nephews Lil Brian (Tonya's son), Lil Brian, Anthony, LeBryant, Baby B, and Khari, as well as all the rest of my family and my two guys Fat Kev and Boss Hog (Free both of them!!!)

Last, but far from least, R.I.H. TO MY GRANNY! WITHOUT HER NONE OF THE FAMILY MEMBERS I THANKED WOULD EVEN BE HERE. She passed away while I was writing this book; so Granny it took me forever but I finally did something with myself. I said without Granny my family wouldn't be here, but without God she wouldn't have been here, so thank you so much to Him. I know your Grace is real because I'm a living example of it. With that, I'm in traffic!!!

Introduction

My name is Joseph Majors and I'm a convicted felon residing in Wabash Valley Correctional Facility. Writing this book was never a dream or passion of mine, but more of a challenge laid out by my older sister Shar'ron. She has written two books and has always preached to me, anything she has accomplished, I can too. I brushed off the idea for about three years because I didn't want to write a book about change when I was still conducting myself as the same person who ended up in prison. Most of my life, I allowed my emotions and behavior to override my intellect in a detrimental way; hence me being incarcerated. So one day in November of 2020, someone pissed me off so bad that I was about to yet again do something stupid, but instead I caught myself and said this is your moment to change. So I called my mother and told her, I'm finally going to let my anger turn into a positive. Now I had to convince my sister I was serious because I've disappointed her so many times in the past with my lies about change. I began to write her a chapter a day until it turned into: *Reflection: Change Starts with YOU!* See, the main thing prison has taught me is, no person, circumstance, or ordeal can change a person, only the person they see in the mirror everyday can get the transformation started. It doesn't matter what new opportunity is bestowed upon a person if their habits don't change to match what it takes to maximize that opportunity. So I wrote this book to hopefully help a person who struggles to find the motivation, desire, or courage to put the nonsense behind them and open themselves up to a better way of living. With that being said, I hope reading this helps you as much as writing it helped me.

Contents

Chapter 1: Evolve

I want to start this book off with evolving, because if you're reading this book, then you're already showing that you've got the ability to do just that. Evolution is a pillar of change and success. Being rigid or stubborn will only hinder your growth and leave you far behind the pack. Let's use the great Henry Ford as an example. He was the founder and CEO of Ford Motor Company. He had a vision for an eight cylinder vehicle with everything in one engine block. This was unheard of at the time. He and his engineers eventually hit with the Model T. This car would not only change the world, but bring him vast wealth beyond his belief. But in his success, he became bullheaded and allowed his competition to catch up to him because as successful as the Model T was there's always someone working to come up with the next big thing. That is exactly what happened. Chrysler, GMC, and Dodge were all able to make cars that were better than the Model T because Henry Ford refused to yield to change and was stuck in the past. It took for his wife to force him to give control of the company to their son in order for the company to survive. See, change doesn't only apply to negative results, but positive ones too. When you refuse to evolve you're refusing to ever admit that you're wrong. Now, you show me somebody who always thinks they're right and I'll show you a fool. Think about how beautiful evolution is. Look at how far cars, communication, homes, and everything else in the world has come. Can you imagine still traveling by horse and buggy? Or sending mail by carrier pigeon? Even being incarcerated, these tablets changed the game. Before this, you still had to wait in line to use a pay phone in the joint. Let that sink in. It's 2018 and you're still using a pay phone. That's what your life is without evolving. You're a pay phone instead of that new iPhone or Galaxy. As Colin Cowherd says, "When you say it out loud, it doesn't even sound right."

"It's never too late to change, so I won't let my past hinder my future."

Chapter 2: Open Mind

A key part of evolving is having an open mind. By simply being open to new experiences, challenges, and ideas, you can begin to make drastic positive strides in your life. Now, think about a time you had your mind set on going somewhere only to get there and find out it's closed. Doesn't that just throw you off? You'll experience that feeling constantly if you live a close minded life. Only you won't be missing out on a sale or good time, but all the great things life has to offer you will just pass you by. I use to be a real picky eater as an adolescent and my mama use to always tell me, boy take a no thank you bite. That's the mentality you've got to wake up with everyday. You can't knock something you've never even given a chance. Know what I think about when someone is set in their ways and doesn't want to try a new experience… REGRETS! Do you really want to live life full of should've, could've, wish I would've? I know JoJo doesn't! I can never understand how a person can grow up in a horrible environment or was parented in a way that they knew was wrong, but when they get the opportunity to change it they don't and they just continue that negative cycle. It's because way too often we condition our minds to be closed off to possibilities outside of what we see growing up on a day to day basis. I love cliché sayings that have been around forever because they all hold true. When things aren't going right just tell yourself, out with the old, in with the new. Being closed minded is congruent to being insane and I'm tired of wearing that label. What about you?

"I won't say no, without giving it a go."

Chapter 3: Self Awareness

The ability to be self-aware is pivotal when trying to go from destructive to constructive! It shows you've got the understanding to be realistic about where or who you are in life. Too many times we want people to view us as we think we are instead of what we are actually displaying to the world. Being self aware takes you being honest with yourself about your weaknesses. Say you're of high intellect and are business savvy, but you have a long and extensive history of drug abuse. Now, at no point in your life have you shown the ability to stay clean, but you've got an incredible business plan for a chain of grocery stores, in an area in need. Everyone you're pitching your idea to keeps turning you down for the capital to get your plan off the ground. Not because they don't believe in your business plan, but because they don't believe in your ability to stay clean. Every time you are rejected, you run back to your buddies you get high with looking for a pity party, portraying your dilemma as people not believing in your vision, instead of being honest with yourself; that your addiction is what has everyone hesitant to invest in you. This is a complete lack of self-awareness and as long as you stay in this state of mind, success will always be out of your grasp. In order to alleviate yourself of this frame of mind, you've got to be willing to give yourself a reality check! The best way to do this is by being completely honest with yourself. Trust me I know how hard this can be, especially when you're not in the position you want to be in life, but it's the only way you can stop living a fairy tale. And as we all know, fairy tales aren't real. So if you want people to view you in a better light, then be self aware enough to know what needs to change about your life, so you can begin to work your way out of those dark places.

"Every day I wake up I'll be truthful about where I'm at in life so I can get to where I want to be."

Chapter 4: Accountable

In order to be accountable, you have to acknowledge that what you did was wrong and actually want to do what it takes to make it right! In the society we live in today, everyone wants to blame someone else for their shortcomings. Not to say that there isn't oppression and prejudice, but we can't let that impede us from success. Every day you wake up is an opportunity to be better than the day before. If you consciously decide to make a decision that can impact your life in a detrimental way, you've got to take accountability for that. At the end of the day your life is just that, YOUR LIFE! Don't allow abuse from others, a lack of love or support to be your reason for continuing down the wrong path. One thing to always remember that can keep you staying strong is whatever you've been through or are going through, someone else has been in that predicament too. Take the initiative to look for the ones who turned lemons into lemonade and didn't sit around sulking over their disadvantages! As my mama says, "You can't let them steal your joy." That will only allow negative energy to constantly permeate through your mind, body, and soul and when has that ever been productive? Instead, use your pain as a tool to help the next person not to feel the pain you felt. The blame game has never gotten anybody anywhere. You can't turn your life around unless you're willing to take responsibility for everything in it.

"No more excuses! I'm 100% accountable for all the decisions in my life."

Chapter 5: Focus

Now we're getting to the part you've really got to embrace in your turn around. Focus is the keys to the car. You can have nice paint, chrome rims, V-12 engine and leather insides, but if you don't have the keys, you're not going anywhere! It's the exact same concept when you live a life without a singular focus. SO many people live a life lacking of peace of mind that focusing on a task that leads to success seems impossible. At the end of the day focus is what separates the 1-percenters from the rest of us. Lebron, Serena, Oprah all had one focus they honed in on and once they mastered that, it allowed them to expand their portfolios beyond belief. It amazes me how many people spend their time in someone else's business when they could focus that time on establishing a business. Ownership is the ultimate goal in life and you can't accomplish that worrying about anything outside of being great. If we had the same focus for chasing a career opportunity or obtaining a college degree as we apply to detrimental, frivolous, and counterproductive actions there's no telling how far we could go. Focus starts from laying out goals and creating a plan to help you execute said goals.

Focus is the epitome of steering yourself in the right direction. Focus is the difference between living to die and dying to live. So which side of the fence do you want to stay on? I know where I stand.

"Distractions will no longer rule my day, because staying FOCUSED is the only WAY!"

Chapter 6: Sacrifice

Now before I go any further, I feel this chapter is as good as any to address something I feel needs to be said. When you read this, don't think I'm writing from a vantage point of judgment or with a lack of empathy. No. This is me speaking from my experiences trying to touch your soul and let you know that it's never too late to get your life in order. So now it's time to get into why sacrificing is so important. Trust me I know how easy it is to make everything about you; I've been selfish for 33 years. Playing victim and always wanting people to see it your way, but guess what, that mentality will get you nowhere, but thrown away. Take me writing this book, I'm doing this for my older sister who has given to me ten times over and has never asked for anything in return. She has written two books and if she thinks I can get published, why not give her some material to shop around. It's the least I can do for all of the heartache I have caused her. Yet she still believes in me to the extent that she thinks I can become a published author. Now take my mother, she gave a lawyer $7,500 to represent me while I fought a murder and attempted murder case. This was exactly 10 years ago. Not one time has that woman brought it up, threw it in my face, or made me feel like I owe her anything. Not to mention I'm writing this as I sit in Wabash Valley Correctional Facility for a separate Attempted Murder Case. So, her sacrifice was in vain because I put myself in the exact same position after I came out of the first situation. By the way, my sister gave the lawyer the other $2,500 and looked me in the eyes and said all she wanted in return was for me to get my life together. It took me having a child and being in prison for the past 9 years to fully understand what it took for them to do that for me. Life is about all the moments you can put smiles on other people's faces and times you can motivate or impact someone else in a positive way. When you give without expecting in return, it shows a sense of self-assurance most people don't have. Next time you're thinking of taking away from somebody, give instead and watch the type of energy it brings to your life!

"My life is no longer about personal gain, but how I can help enrich others."

Chapter 7: Love

Now, it's time to address love. It's such a complicated emotion. To be truthful, I believe far too many people have never truly been loved, therefore they don't know how to love themselves nor other people. This, in turn, begins and continues a cycle of distrust, deceit, manipulation, and many other negative precedents. A life without love can never be a life worth living. Lacking love means you never experience happiness, empathy, care, or understanding for wanting to be better. Think about it. If you don't love your job, how can it turn into a productive career? If you don't love life how can you be there for the person or people you don't even know will need you in your lifetime. If you don't properly love your kids how can you teach them to go further than you in life? It took me having a child, a daughter at that; ask any man it's different than having a son, to fully understand what it means to love. How she'll let a man talk to her depends on how I love her. How confident she'll approach tasks in her life depends on my love. The way she absorbs and bounces back from adversity depends on the love she gets from me. Because if I don't love her properly as she grows into whom she'll become in life, why should I expect her to require it of herself and others? The love our children receive plays a pertinent part in how they excel or crumble in life. We've got to love ourselves in order to be able to love each other! Self love creates love that can pass along to the next person. And that's a big step of breaking the divisive cycle we find ourselves in today.

"Love is the key that unlocks all that life has to offer."

Chapter 8: Money Management

This chapter is less about the type of emotions it takes to improve your life and more about a very important skill set you need for change. That's money management. Far too many of us are financially ignorant. We either were never taught the true value of money or never took the time to actually pay attention and learn how to handle cash. Hill Harper had a quote in his book *Letters to an Incarcerated Brother* that stood out to me about money. He said, so many people think getting a lot of money is the end all, be all, when in fact, money is just a tool and if not used properly, won't fix any of your problems. I'll die living by that statement. I classify people who dispense their funds carelessly as having spontaneous finances. I know you're reading that laughing like, I've never heard someone describe a person's handling of money as spontaneous. That's my point exactly; you should never fall under that umbrella. I'll get into this more in a later chapter, but you've got to learn the power of the long game. It's important to find that balance of wanting a lot of money, but also having a well thought out purpose for this desire. Too many of us don't even sit down and really go over our books. You've got to establish how much money you'll net each month. Then calculate how much all your bills come up to, plus your necessities. This includes gas and food, which you can't go without. You always want to keep something to the side for unforeseen circumstances such as unexpected car maintenance. If you've got children, money management is even more imperative. Their expenses will range anywhere from childcare to doctor visits. I know keeping the latest technology and shoes look better on social media, but it can't feel good always having to rob Peter to pay Paul. It's one thing to not have money at all, that's not what I'm talking about. It's another thing to get $10,000 back from your tax return and be broke within a month and having nothing to show for it but a nice T.V. and wardrobe. It's impossible to live a prosperous life when you're always making horrible financial decisions. Think about this, if everybody in the world got a million dollars today, I'd guess only 5% would have a million a year from now. This isn't a "you problem" or "me problem," this is a society problem. We've got to do a better job of becoming cash literate. Always remember what you want should never get confused with what you need.

"I will begin to think, save instead of spend."

Chapter 9: Next Play Mentality

This is a sport's term used in order to get you to not dwell on your failures, but to prepare you for your next achievement. So many times when we're use to things going a certain way or we try something new and it goes bad we tend to sulk or revert back to our old ways. This is a huge NO, NO! Establishing in your mind the next play mentality will allow you to accept failure in a positive way. There's a saying I use, a lose is a lesson, therefore my wins are blessings. When faced with adversity, you've got to embrace it and learn to move forward. No one who has ever achieved something great did it on their first attempt. To me, the beginning of developing this frame of mind is realizing, every day that you wake up is a chance for you to be better than the day before. My mama always says only the strong can survive and there aren't too many truer statements. Honestly, sometimes it's good to try things even when you know there's a small chance of it succeeding just so you can get the experience and feedback from someone who has done it before. That way the next time you give it a go, you'll be equipped with everything you need to get over the hump.

“I won’t allow my failures of yesterday to stop me from succeeding today.”

Chapter 10: Faith

Let's enter into a conversation about something a lot of people struggle with and that's faith. Before you assume I'm about to be speaking strictly in a holy sense, just know that you've got to have faith to prosper in a secular based lifestyle too. Faith for me isn't just about God, but about believing you can achieve what most deem impossible. You know why so many people from impoverished areas continue to struggle generation after generation? Lack of faith. As humans, far too often, if we can't see it, we don't believe it. Trust me when I tell you that this should never be the case. Martin Luther King Jr. said faith is taking a step when you don't know what lies ahead. That's the type of mindset I want to approach life with. We can't allow ourselves to become boxed in or complacent with what's in front of us on a daily basis. We've been given the keys to too many vehicles to not get in and bend a few corners outside of our own neighborhoods. You can't become a great athlete by only competing against the people from your own neighborhood, you've got to have faith that your skills can transition across the world before you even step into those gyms. Nobody can be recognized as an elite chef only cooking in their local diner. Naw, you've got to have faith that you can cook Rachel Ray out of business before you ever step in a kitchen with her. Faith is the great equalizer. See, when your faith is strong your mind is strong and nothing or no one can deter you from your dreams. A person full of faith is the most unstoppable person you can encounter. This is how you know when their faith is strong, they're always optimistic. Everybody at the office hates the boss because he or she is always grouchy, but your coworker who is full of faith always manages to get a daily laugh out of them. Everybody is looking like how they do that? The faithful person just takes it in stride. There's good in us all. We've just got to have the faith to seek it out of each other. Always remember, what you haven't seen is what you may have always been in need of. You've just got to have faith in yourself to go out and get it.

"Faith is the tool I'll use to fix what is broken in my life."

Chapter 11: Long Game

I referenced the long game in an earlier chapter, but now it's time to delve all the way into it. Applying this frame of mind to your life is crucial because most times when we fail it's because we're chasing microwave success. Just like when you're preparing a meal, the food that tastes the best, is the food that we take our time preparing. It's the same with how you live your life. You can't take a steak out the freezer, pop it in the microwave and think it's going to become a gourmet meal. It's going to be raw and unprepared; headed straight for the trash. The same thing is going to happen to anything in life you try to rush through while executing. Have you ever honestly sat down and said to yourself, I don't care if it takes ten years to do something; I just want to get it done? No you haven't. Why, because most people are built to think if something takes ten years to do, it's not worth doing. And that's where those people have it wrong. I read a report recently from a stock investment group. They said if you would've invested $1,000 in Netflix, Amazon, Google, and one other company at the time they told you to, those investments would be worth $616,000 right now. That's the power of the long game. Instead, we'd rather take $1,000 and buy a leather coat that's only going to be in style for one winter. Or go to the club and ball out. That's the microwave game. Ohh I can touch it right now. Truthfully, it's the way children think. But mommy I want it now. I don't know about you, but I'm 33. I'm too old to be thinking like my 8 year old daughter. Everything we break our necks to buy from the latest phone, car, video game and whatever else you can think of came from the long game. You don't think it's crazy that you're willing to splurge on the long game year after year for entertainment, but won't make a real investment you can see a financial return on down the road?

"I'm through living for just today, so I can begin to prepare for tomorrow."

Chapter 12: Educate Yourself

Let me start off by saying accepting being ignorant is not cool and in my opinion, is unacceptable. It always blows my mind how many of us will venture off into a new endeavor without the proper knowledge and then really play like we don't know why we failed! Please people, you've got to educate yourself before you can even begin to think about accomplishing anything worth setting out to do. LL Cool J said, "Once you make it big and those checks start to come in, the first thing you need to do is surround yourself with people who are smarter than you." I love this concept, but let me add this, don't do this so you can be lazy and let someone else do all the work for you. Because all that will end up happening is they'll see you're not as knowledgeable as you should be and you'll get taken advantage of. Surround yourself with these people so every day is like a teaching seminar. They're not lying when they say we learn something new every day, but are you putting yourself in position to be taught? As a kid I always remember people saying they can never take your brain from you. I honestly didn't understand the significance of this until I received a letter from my brother while we both were incarcerated. He's going to be pissed I put this in here, but so what, it's my book and he stays telling embarrassing stories about me. So he was struggling to pass the GED test (he has it now) and it had been over 4 years since he had started school. So he was like, man bro, I can't get a damn 400! Like a 400, this is ridiculous. Mind you, school has never been bro's thing. He's always been in the streets. So I'm really feeling for him through his letter. Now fast forward a year later, I'm 5 ½ years into my bid, but I haven't gotten my GED either, because I was too busy playing in the joint. Mind you, I was the opposite of bro, always an honor roll student. I was 90 days from being 30 years old so I said, let me quit playin' and knock this out real quick. At the time I hadn't been to school in 11 years. I take the test to see where you're at and got all 12.9, which is the highest you can get. So the teacher is looking at me like, *why the hell are you locked up*? Then the teacher was like, there's a qualifier the day after tomorrow and if you pass that we have the actual GED test scheduled for next Tuesday and Wednesday. To make a long story short I was only in school for 8 days and it only took that long because they only test once they have a certain amount of people who have passed the qualifier in the joint. My point is your brain is the most lethal possession God blessed you with, so keep it sharp!

"Before I can act, I've got to be able to think."

Chapter 13: Urgency

Let me establish a premise in this chapter. I'm not your typical author. So there's going to be times when I come off as abrasive and I just want you to know, it comes from a place of love and understanding for your struggles, but at the same time, I'm not with enabling people's lackluster behavior. Now, let us get into urgency and the importance of it. As I've gotten older it has become abundantly clear to me that I don't vibe with nonchalant people on any level or with individuals who build their lives around procrastinating. Life is too short to not maximize each and every day. So if a person isn't as passionate about learning, prosperity, and overall growth as me, we'll never mesh. I can hear you now, but what about the long game? Yeah, I did speak on the importance of the long game, but you can only utilize the long game when you have urgency on positioning yourself to be able to apply the long game. Ever heard of the saying, "time waits for no one?" It's been around for generations for a reason. People who seize moments and make the most of them are the people life considers the 1-percenters. Having positive urgency is the best way for a person to stop being an individual sitting around idle letting the devil occupy their mind. Urgency gives you the mindset to never settle and to always keep a forward thinking perspective. When we stay stuck in the same place, we tend to go backwards and we all know that going backwards leads us to facing the same problems.

"I'll treat today like my last and when the opportunity presents itself I'll jump on it fast."

Chapter 14: Organization

Being organized allows you to maximize your life both figuratively and literally. We all know someone who is always looking for something because their house is always a mess or who is constantly frustrated because they put too many things on their plate with no structure to get them done. One of the most important things being organized eliminates from your life is being late. Organized people are always well prepared, early, and eager to accomplish the task. Next, being organized will help you keep a clean, well thought out lifestyle. Why do we keep things we'll never use, wear, or in some cases even open? Or focus on the things that add no value to our existence? Organization will remove all that clutter from your home and brain and watch all the space you'll create for actual things of use. Organization gives a person the best chance to be in position to get the most done. When you put everything in its proper place it reduces the chances of your life being out of order. Finally, organization enables you to become the most efficient version of yourself and in 2021 that's what separates the haves from the have-nots.

“Organization puts everything in my life in perspective so I can’t be tripped up by loose ends.”

Chapter 15: Efficient

So I ended the last chapter on organization by bringing up efficiency and how it separates the haves from the have-nots. See if you're not efficient in your life then you're not getting the most out of your life. In all walks of life, that's what everyone is looking for, how can I invest the least in something or someone and get the most return with the lowest risk. Let's take it to the basketball court. Say I score 30 points in a game; most people would say I had a hell of a game. What I didn't say was it took me 30 shots to get those 30 points, that's beyond inefficient. You want to be the person who can put up 30 on 16 shots, that's a more efficient night. How often do people say, "If only there was more time in the day?" Why? So you can just have more hours to waste? An efficient person can do in 20 minutes what the next person takes an hour to do. How can you become your apex self when you go to bed every night knowing that you didn't do the most you could with your day? If you spend just as much time on social media or more, for free, as you do working, this is a huge sign of inefficiency. Break your life down into a chart based on percentages. Everyone's life is different so I'll use work, school, kids, and relaxing as examples. On this list if relaxing is anywhere close in percentages to those other 3 that's why your days aren't as productive as they should be.

"Time to put 100% into success, therefore I give 0% to any mess."

Chapter 16: Support

I'm telling you, if you're not truly trying to get yourself together, put my words down because you're either not going to be able to stand me or you're not going to understand me. Either way, this book isn't for you. This is for the individuals who are truly trying to go from a destitute mindset to a frame of mind of prosperity and appreciation for the blessing of being able to be better every day they wake up. So take a trip with me. Support is the destination. Support elevates minds, saves lives, and is one of the purest forms of love. Without the support I've gotten over the last nine years, I don't know how I would be making it through my situation. The constant mental and emotional strength you've got to exert each day to stay strong and sane in prison is indescribable. My support system has too many names to list, but it's everybody from my mother to my daughter and everybody in between. So let me focus on two people in particular: my mother and sister. I told you at the beginning, I'm residing at Wabash Valley Correctional Facility. My conviction is attempted murder, but 18 months before I caught this case, I was blessed to have a murder and attempted murder case dismissed. On that case, my mother and sister put $10,000 together to hire a lawyer for me. And how did I repay them; by still ending up with 45 years in prison. Even with that egregious act of ungratefulness those two women still stand by me 100%. They answer the phone practically every time I call and are always there when I need help with my daughter. They never throw anything in my face; all they do is constantly give me positive reinforcement, so how could I not write this book for them. How could I say I was going to be different when I was refusing to write this book my sister kept asking me to? What better way to make my mother proud than to take the time to put my words to use for the betterment of people instead of using my words and actions to keep being destructive. See, it was their support that gave me the drive to rise above my circumstances and do something constructive with my time. You are what you surround yourself with. If you choose to stay mingling with people who have a dead-end mindset, you'll never go anywhere. But if you stay close to people who are willing to give you the tools you need, you'll be able to fix any problem life brings you.

"I'll surround myself with strength so I can constantly fight my weaknesses."

Chapter 17: Resist

Our inability to resist detrimental urges is honestly probably the most overlooked flaw that we struggle with. Think about how many people on a daily basis spend money they know they don't have; always putting their wants before their needs! For what? To look good for someone else, who's only going to find something else to dog you out about anyway? Or when people constantly go back to dealing with the same person, knowing the relationship is beyond toxic. It's always, "but I love him," even though he hits her. "Bro look how good she looks," but she loves his money more than him. A person with uncontrollable urges will always find themselves in a hole moving backwards. Whether it's getting high, gambling, or sex, it doesn't matter; doing these things constantly will get you nowhere. We've got to put ourselves in situations where our only urge is to be successful. To combat an urge you've got to identify your triggers and then utilize the support we talked about. Instead of succumbing to the urge as you usually do, pick up the phone and call someone who can help you. See, pride goes hand and hand with this. I can guarantee you people who struggle with resisting also struggle with pride, because they always think they've got it under control, until it's too late. Pride has you thinking you don't have a problem and that there is always time to figure it out. Let me tell you that there isn't always time. Time waits for no one. So the next time you get the urge to do something you know isn't in your best interest, take a moment to realize, this may be the last time you get.

"My only urge will be to try to be better than yesterday."

Chapter 18: Let it Go

I don't have any statistics or data, but I swear that dwelling on the negative things we can't change has to be one of the top 10 causes of death. It is so counterproductive to excelling in life. I got into an argument with my brother the other day, even though he tried to call it a conversation, and I'm still sitting here talking to myself about it. Like, how crazy is that. We're both in prison, fighting for our lives and I'm sitting here frustrated about last week. That type of thinking is what causes people to waste 10 years of their life without even realizing it. You're so busy worried about yesterday that you can't focus on today, let alone building towards your future. See, as I'm writing this I'm not speaking down to you or judging, I'm speaking from my own decisions, flaws, and day to day struggles. A person who can't truly address, resolve, and move forward is a person who doesn't want to go anywhere. They love being stuck in those negative moments. Right now together let's breathe all of our junk in and exhale it out, so we can move on to bigger and better things.

"Today I will stop holding on so I can begin to let go."

Chapter 19: Balance

Something I had to share my take on is the importance of being balanced. When you're looking to change your life and become the peak version of yourself, don't overlook balance. We can keep it simple and say, when things aren't balanced properly; they do what? They fall over and break. The only things we want to break are negative cycles and behaviors. If you notice, most times when people are use to things being a certain way, and that way isn't necessarily healthy; they get the thought to change it, but they can't keep the momentum for change because of their lack of balance. If you've been eating unhealthy all your life, you shouldn't then try an all liquid diet off top to lose weight. It's too drastic of a switch that will have you feeling so overwhelmed that it's only a matter of time before you revert back to what you're used to. Especially if you don't get those instant results. Remember the long game and how we fall prey to microwave success. Remaining balanced throughout the process of you getting your life in order is key because everything and everyone from your past isn't bad. Once you begin to become a new person, you don't want to develop the mindset that you've got it all figured out and now you can go around constantly judging people. That will only turn people off and create negative feelings in you, thinking that people are hating on you. Now instead of you remaining focused on the positive you're back with constant counterproductive thoughts. Staying neutral and keeping things in perspective will always keep you even keel.

"Remaining balanced is the key to getting my life in order from all angles."

Chapter 20: Persistence

My sis told me a few weeks ago, "Bro, good, bad or indifferent you are persistent." I swear just today I asked her to put some debit links on my tablet and reminded her four times and we were only on the phone for about seven minutes. I guess I can't object to her assessment. Plus, I embrace never letting up. I don't believe in taking 'no' for an answer or giving up because I fail the first time when I'm trying to get something done. Tying your boots up and continuing to power through is essential to change. You've got to be able to meet adversity head on and plow through it like a shovel in the snow. Being persistent will get doors opened that others say have long been closed. Persistence gets you over the top when everyone around you can't make it up the hill. It's having the mindset of, if there's a will, there's a way. It's crucial to change because it allows true grit to permeate through you. Stop and think about everyone who has achieved the unthinkable; it was persistence that helped steer them through. How else do you think they were able to block out the naysayers or see the ways to success that others had overlooked? Persistence allows you to say I don't like something going on in my life and I'll stop at nothing to eliminate it. It gives you the comfort to know that no matter what, you've got the strength to pull it all together.

"Let persistence be the flame that lights your change."

Chapter 21: Self Evaluation

How often do you look in the mirror or sit down and have a real conversation with yourself about where you're at in life? In today's time, there is so much emphasis put on the importance of maintaining a sound state of mental health. So are you doing your part and being honest with yourself on a daily basis? I'm asking because they say if a person tells a lie enough times that lie becomes that person's truth. And there's absolutely no way an individual can make positive strides if they're not keeping it real from within. That's why daily self-evaluation is so important. You have to identify those areas in your life that are counterproductive to success and eliminate them. We can put on a facade for others all we want, but when you go home at the end of the night and have to live with your reality, the truth will eat at you. Lying to others in "some" instances hurts them but will always hurt the person doing the lying. Being truthful about your status in life will only help you realize where you're lacking and what you need to add and subtract to get to the solutions of your problems. It's crazy how we'll take inventory of our refrigerators, closets, and technology, but won't take inventory of the things that cause us to be destructive, indecisive, and unproductive. Taking the time to have an honest conversation with yourself everyday will take you to places you've been searching for and didn't even realize you had the power to get to your whole life.

"Daily self-evaluation will eliminate those self-inflicted wounds."

Chapter 22: Words

Whether it's what you say or how you say it, words are so powerful. I've already addressed why I'm in prison, but to tell the truth I've hurt more people mentally and emotionally than I have physically. I was the definition of a hurt person who wanted to hurt in return. Man, if you lack proper communication when things aren't going your way, you'll get nowhere in life. People will never forget when you talked to them like they never meant anything to you. It'll have them scared to be themselves around you or to be honest with you if they disagree with you on an issue. There's no way any of that will help you change for the better. People not wanting to have a genuine dialogue with you for fear of you using your words as weapons will only hinder your progress in life. If you struggle with this, first, you need to reach out to anyone that you care about and that you know cares about you and apologize. Admit where you were wrong and whether or not you get the response you're looking for remain sincere and cordial. Next, you need to understand that it may be best for you that once you get angry you shut your mouth and remove yourself from the conversation to prevent ruining any relationship because of this moving forward.

You don't want to be the person known for being petty, vindictive, and small minded. You want to bring joy, encouragement, and love to people with what you have to say. Remember words have a lasting effect on people so make sure what you have to say has a positive impact when you speak.

"Keep it simple. If you don't have anything nice to say, don't say anything at all."

Chapter 23: Anger Equals Creation

I want you to think about all the times you allowed your anger to control your decision making. It doesn't matter if you used hurtful words, physically harmed someone, or destroyed property. Just imagine if you used that same energy to create a potential positive opportunity for yourself instead of an impediment. I touched on this before, but the same energy you use to be destructive is the same energy it would take for you to become productive. See what we fail to realize is so many of the people we admire, support, and strive to live life like were motivated by anger. Success is built off of anger, doubt and frustration. Just imagine how many times Oprah was told a female couldn't dominate daytime TV. Or even after she proved that theory wrong how often she was told that she would never be able to create and sustain her own TV network. She didn't allow the anger she must have felt to deter her. Instead she used it as fuel to become the wealthiest black woman in the world. Now take Serena and Venus; how many nights do you think they went home pissed as two young black females trying to break into the tennis community. With all the racial slurs being hurled at them and constant judgment about their physical appearances, they could have easily allowed that anger they were feeling to be the reason for them to give up. Instead they used it to become two of the greatest to ever pick up a tennis racket. Serena is arguably the greatest female tennis player ever. Not just in the tennis community, but these women are inspirations for so many people who grew up, look like, and were made to feel like them when they were coming up trying to become somebody. See, you can't allow anger to be what wrecks your life and takes you off course. We've been taught to associate anger with negativity, but it's not the anger that's bad. It's a person who loses self control when angry that's the problem. Allow your anger to be what propels your solutions instead of your problems!

"My anger will no longer destroy, but be what brings my life joy."

Chapter 24: Learn to Say 'No'

It was during my sentencing hearing for the case I'm currently incarcerated for when I got hit with the realest "no" I've ever heard. My sister that I've been referencing throughout this book is a devout Christian and it was on that day I found out how dedicated to God she truly is. I was attempting to get people together to speak on my behalf in hopes of getting my sentence mitigated and it's safe to say the mitigation didn't happen! Anyway, my lawyer came to me and said your sister says she refuses to speak on your behalf because it's her understanding that you did commit this crime and she will not break her principles to lie for your potential benefit. I know a lot of people would have felt a type of way, but honestly at that point I was numb to everything around me. See, unbeknownst to my sister, she taught me a valuable lesson that day and that was the power of saying "no". Again if you look at the chapters on support and sacrifice, she's been there for me throughout my entire 33 years on this earth and on top of that I really believe that's the first time she ever told me "no" when I asked for something from her. Now, I'm not saying it immediately changed me or I had an epiphany or anything, but that moment has never left me. Think about all the times you've lost money, wasted time, or felt used all because you said "yes". When we have love for people, so many times we throw reason and rationale out the window just trying to be there for someone. When nine times out of ten that person isn't there for themselves, so you know if the role was reversed, they couldn't be there for you. A lot of the time tough love is the best love. When you lack the ability to say "no" and it comes back to slap you in the face, this only wears on you and then you're putting yourself in a bad mental space and that's never good. Just remember if it's really love, then the person should know you're telling them "no" for a reason!

"Sometimes it's in your best interest to just say "no"."

Chapter 25: Significant Lover

I know, you read the chapter title, like "doesn't he mean significant other?" Naw, because if it's the type of relationship I'm talking about you want that love attached to it. Where I'm from, we're not speaking positively of you if we say "you on some other stuff anyway." Seriously though, let's focus on the word significant. The first thing that comes to my mind when I think of the word significant is important so that's what I'll begin with. A lot of us are or have been in a very, very unimportant relationship and were lying to ourselves about how great a situation it was or is. When your other is insignificant how can they possibly help you be the best you? At the end of the day we can talk and put on a brave face all we want, but when we go to bed at night or look in that mirror we know the truth about the relationship, even if we refuse to come to grips with it. That's why it's important not to settle or get trapped because of love and circumstances. See a real significant lover is just that, a person who puts a premium on the love at all times and in those tough moments is trying to figure out how to get the relationship back in that comfortable position for the both of y'all.

Your significant lover should be strong when you're weak. When you're tired, they have the ability to hit their peak. Significant lovers provide that balance I was talking about. When you've got this type of person in your corner you know what it is at all times. A woman I love very much said something to me that has really stuck with me. I told her to always remember the date, December 18th because that's the morning she said it to me. She said she wants that thing where can't nobody tell her nothing about what we've got going on. It stuck out to me because I know too many women that refuse to leave a man who if somebody told them he was cheating they wouldn't be surprised. Or if he came home and put his hands on her it would just be another day. This type of mindset has to change in order for you to be able to truly love yourself. Don't allow anyone or anything to have you feeling insignificant.

"If the love isn't significant then what's the significance of the relationship?"

Chapter 26: Mean Mentality

They just put a podcast app on our tablets this week and one of the podcasts happens to be hosted by Questlove from the Roots. There was an episode featuring Gabrielle Union and she was speaking about a speech she had given at the Essence Awards when she received an award. She said she spoke about having that mean girl mentality and wishing ill on other actresses for no reason other than to prop herself up. I ran this past my sister and she said this was called a "lacking" mentality. Feeling like things weren't in abundance. As soon as she said it, it clicked to me, how debilitating of a mindset this could be for someone to develop. Coming from the streets this type of mindset leads to a lot of premeditated murders. You're robbing and killing someone solely based on them possessing something you don't have. Then you end up with all day in prison for doing something to someone that in most cases doesn't even know you. Then I think about the corporate world; this thinking can hurt a company's bottom line. When you've got in-fighting and people not fully supporting one other, how can you possibly get everyone's best on a product? This mentality prohibits your ability to see that by encouraging and supporting someone else's success you open more doors for yourself and the ones who come after you. Really, think about all the energy it takes to wish ill on someone for no reason at all. In order for all of us to get to where we want in life, we've got to understand that we're not always going to be the one to get through the door first. That doesn't mean it'll be locked by the time we get there. We've just got to be ready to move in once we get our set of keys.

"Remember, negative thoughts eventually lead to negative actions."

Chapter 27: Happiness

What I've learned during my 33 years on this Earth is it's easier to reflect, determine, and accomplish when you know what makes you happy. So many of us lack any type of joy on a daily basis. I believe they call it going through the motions. It's one of the main reasons I wrote this book because it's hard for me to look in the mirror when I know happiness is lacking in my life. When happiness is lacking, it allows anger, denial, and laziness to become in abundance and we all know those attributes have never gotten anything worth noting done. My mother always tells me to find a reason to laugh through all situations no matter how bad the circumstances have me upset. Just think about how often you don't see people smiling. Or how quick we are to hop on a negative current, but only give a positive one a millisecond of our time. Being incarcerated you've got to get creative when looking for happiness. It's similar to when you were a kid and you are constantly using your imagination to take you to places some deem unattainable. I truly feel as a whole our society has either lived in sorrow or faked happiness for so long that most of us don't even know where to begin when looking for it. If your granny went through a lot of trauma as a child, naturally her kids will in turn. Then, we experience trauma ourselves and next thing you know we're putting our children through the same cycles we swore we hated so much as kids. Most, if not all, negative cycle breaking begins with finding what puts a smile on your face. FYI something that can send you to jail, get you fired, or have you embarrassing your family shouldn't put a smile on your face; even though way too many times this is the case. Happiness is the emotion that doesn't allow you to judge, manipulate or be easily bothered. You're so good with who you are when you're truly happy that all you want out of life is for everyone to wake up feeling like you.

"Don't worry, be happy."

Chapter 28: Perseverance

Now a lot of the same ideology that goes into being persistent applies to perseverance, so I'm going to focus on particular aspects of life to distinguish between the two. A large portion of people struggle with change because they were hindered in life before they ever even understood what living a life meant. Whether they were sexually abused as a child, thrown into foster care, or lost their parents tragically as babies; these are some of the most extreme reasons people grow up not loving themselves. So when you don't love yourself it's easy to give up on life when things don't go your way. This is where the importance of perseverance comes into play. See, I've never been through any of those obstacles, so I'm not here to mitigate the damage it's had on a person. What I am here to say is you're not alone in your pain and that if you look, there are people who went through what you did, persevered through and became a model of success. Perseverance gives you that strength you need to turn your pain into a tool to not only help yourself, but other people as well. It helps you fight on those days when you're feeling defeated. It's the fuel you need when you think you're out of gas. Perseverance will pick you up when you feel you've got the weight of the world on your back. It's that thing in the back of your mind that's telling you to keep going when everyone and everything in your life is telling you to stop. Without perseverance we can't overcome the things that hold us back and never allow us to move forward. It gives you the ability to smile when you feel there's nothing to be happy about. Perseverance will help you hold on to hope when it feels like everything is slipping away. Listen to me; I struggle with change just as you do, so let's make a pact together. No matter how grim or bleak the circumstances are, we will stay down with perseverance until we're able to come out on top!

"I refuse to give up so easily, constantly taking steps backwards, because I know I've got the strength inside of me to keep moving forward."

Chapter 29: Capital

It occurred to me one day that a main cause of us not making the best decisions is based on us not valuing ourselves properly. We focus so much energy on obtaining materialistic possessions thinking they'll give us a certain image or set us apart, that we neglect our most important asset, ourselves. Most people think of getting money together to invest in a company when they hear the word capital, but I'm talking about self investment. What better way to change and start making the most out of your life than raising internal capital to give you the mindset you need to become a progressive thinker. If you don't value yourself as a high commodity then how do you expect to ever accomplish anything in life? Having high self esteem and worth are pivotal in going from an impoverished life to a prosperous one. It's having the self confidence to say, if there's a problem I'm equipped to fix it. Self capital is more valuable than actual money. I hear you saying, 'Joseph you're losing me with this one', but just hear me out. A person with no sense of self worth, but who has a whole lot of money will do nothing, but just waste that money on what other people deem important and valuable. Just doing things because they can afford to, but with no sense of real purpose. On the flip side, take a person who is financially strapped, but has high personal capital. They have the understanding and grit to know that they can walk into any room, given the chance, and walk out not only in a better position themselves, but the people they just touched are too. See, when your personal capital is high it means you're invaluable. You're constantly thinking of how to make a profit therefore you don't spend time indulging in costly mistakes. This will allow your personal change to turn into actual dollars. Our minds, bodies, and souls are what will be with us no matter what position we're in, so why wouldn't we invest the most in them?

"I'm my greatest asset: therefore, I'll invest something new into myself every day."

Chapter 30: End Game

With all that I've discussed with you in this book what is your end game? What do you want to come from your change? They always say begin with the end in mind! Do you want to change your financial situation? Want a better relationship with your family? Is losing control when you're angry the issue? Struggling with gambling, drugs, or alcohol? Are you an abusive spouse or constant cheater? Whatever things we lack in, it starts with that person you see in the mirror to get it corrected and you can't get started without knowing where you want to end up. When you know what you're actually changing for, it makes it a little easier to put the gear in drive. I associate the end game with having a purpose. When we get to a point of knowing why we're waking up every day it makes those days so much better. When you don't know where you want to end up, you're bound to get lost. What comes with being lost? Fear, frustrations, anger and all the other feelings and thoughts we're trying to rid ourselves of. Starting with the end established makes it easier to figure out the best path to navigate your way there and helps you avoid those traps that enable us to lose our way. You've got to realize I'm writing this from prison, so I'm surrounded by individuals who got lost and will never get the opportunity to find their way back. They were making decisions just based on impulse and no real purpose, therefore the outcome turned into life in prison. I know everyone's poor choices won't have those severe of consequences, but you don't want to lose a job, friend, or money based on you just making decisions on a whim. The most successful people are the ones who honed in on an objective and didn't deviate from it until it was accomplished. So let's take the necessary steps together to get where we want to be in life.

"I'll know where I'm going, then start looking for the keys to help me get there."

Conclusion

Man, I've got to say I honestly can't believe I actually did it. I'm 33 years old and this is the first constructive thing I've ever done in my life. I personally know so many struggles that I touched on in this book because I live them every day. I know what it's like to disappoint everyone around you and also yourself. They say it's never too late to change, so this is my first step in the right direction. Steve Harvey says, "He ain't done with me yet." How true a statement that is when it comes to my life. I just want to be an example to anyone who's put themselves in a messed up predicament, has constant destitute thoughts, or just doesn't know who they are yet; you're not the only one. So never hesitate to seek out help! We are what we surround ourselves with. Never let a bad moment dictate the rest of your life. No matter where you are in life you can always use each day to become better. This was my first time using my anger to create and it feels so much better than doing something dumb that would've placed me on the SHU (Secure Housing Unit). I want to thank anyone who gave me some of their time and I encourage us all to look for ways to change for the better. I'm out!!!

www.ingramcontent.com/pod-product-compliance
Lightning Source LLC
LaVergne TN
LVHW020658100826
845148LV00012B/2544

* 9 7 8 1 7 3 7 4 6 1 7 0 8 *